# CHILDREN'S SONGS

## FOR OCARINA

The ocarina on the front cover is available at www.halleonard.com, item #HL00363749

ISBN 978-1-70517-438-8

Visit Hal Leonard Online at
**www.halleonard.com**

World headquarters, contact:
**Hal Leonard**
7777 West Bluemound Road
Milwaukee, WI 53213
Email: info@halleonard.com

In Europe, contact:
**Hal Leonard Europe Limited**
1 Red Place
London, W1K 6PL
Email: info@halleonardeurope.com

In Australia, contact:
**Hal Leonard Australia Pty. Ltd.**
4 Lentara Court
Cheltenham, Victoria, 3192 Australia
Email: info@halleonard.com.au

# BABY SHARK

OCARINA

Traditional Nursery Rhyme
Arranged by Pinkfong and KidzCastle

# THE BARE NECESSITIES
from THE JUNGLE BOOK

OCARINA

Words and Music by
TERRY GILKYSON

# "C" IS FOR COOKIE

OCARINA

Words and Music by
JOE RAPOSO

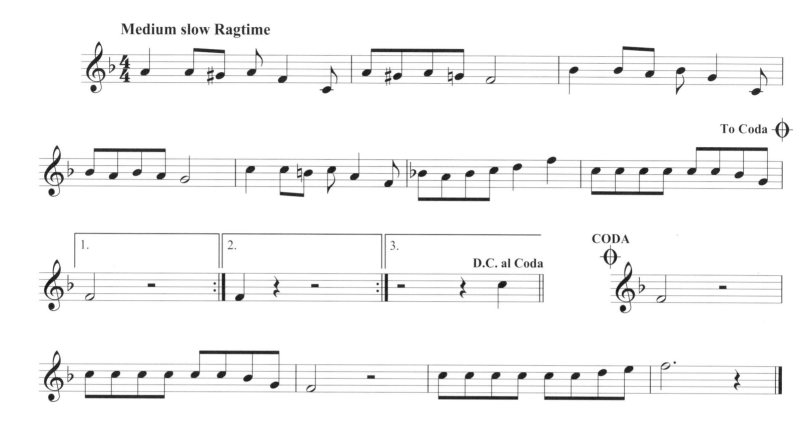

# HAPPY BIRTHDAY TO YOU

Words and Music by MILDRED J. HILL
and PATTY S. HILL

# CAN'T STOP THE FEELING!

from TROLLS

OCARINA

Words and Music by JUSTIN TIMBERLAKE,
MAX MARTIN and SHELLBACK

# CASTLE ON A CLOUD
from LES MISÉRABLES

OCARINA

Music by CLAUDE-MICHEL SCHÖNBERG
Lyrics by ALAIN BOUBLIL, JEAN-MARC NATEL
and HERBERT KRETZMER

# DO-RE-MI
from THE SOUND OF MUSIC

OCARINA

Lyrics by OSCAR HAMMERSTEIN II
Music by RICHARD RODGERS

# DANCE MONKEY

OCARINA

Words and Music by
TONI WATSON

# EVERYTHING IS AWESOME
## (Awesome Remixx!!!)
from THE LEGO MOVIE

OCARINA

Words by SHAWN PATTERSON
Music by ANDREW SAMBERG,
JORMA TACCONE, AKIVA SCHAFFER,
JOSHUA BARTHOLOMEW, LISA HARRITON
and SHAWN PATTERSON

# HAPPY
## from DESPICABLE ME 2

OCARINA

Words and Music by
PHARRELL WILLIAMS

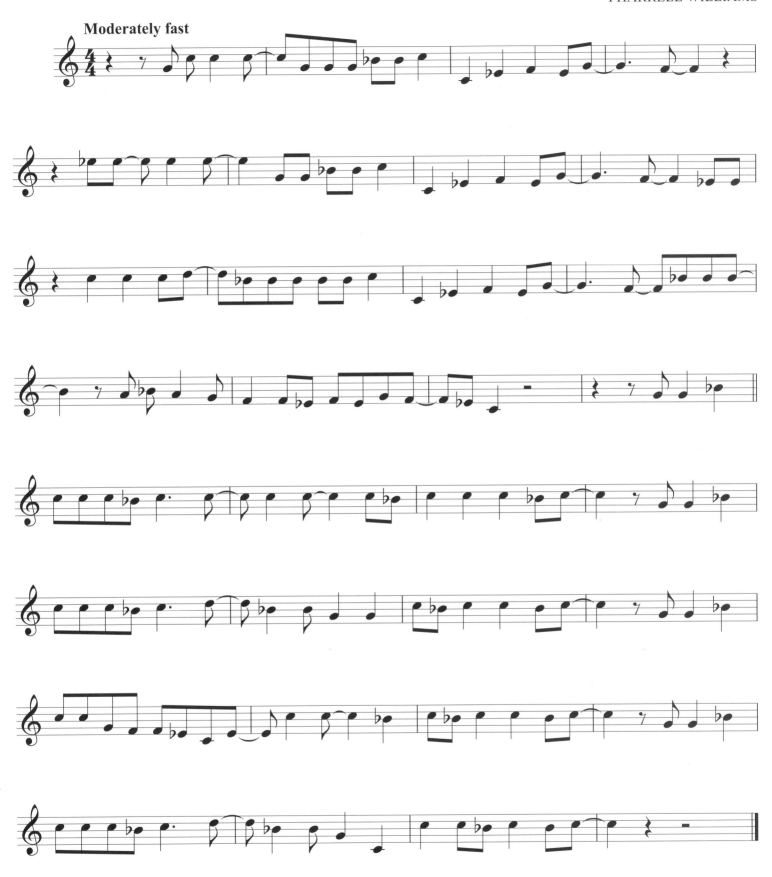

# HEART AND SOUL
from the Paramount Short Subject A SONG IS BORN

OCARINA

Words by FRANK LOESSER
Music by HOAGY CARMICHAEL

# THE HOKEY POKEY

OCARINA

Words and Music by CHARLES P. MACAK,
TAFFT BAKER and LARRY LaPRISE

# IF I ONLY HAD A BRAIN

from THE WIZARD OF OZ

OCARINA

Lyric by E.Y. "YIP" HARBURG
Music by HAROLD ARLEN

# IF YOU'RE HAPPY AND YOU KNOW IT

OCARINA

Words and Music by
L. SMTIH

# YOU ARE MY SUNSHINE

Words and Music by
JIMMIE DAVIS

# IMAGINE

OCARINA

Words and Music by
JOHN LENNON

# IT'S A SMALL WORLD

from Disney Parks' "it's a small world" attraction

OCARINA

Words and Music by RICHARD M. SHERMAN
and ROBERT B. SHERMAN

# THE LAZY SONG

OCARINA

Words and Music by BRUNO MARS,
ARI LEVINE, PHILIP LAWRENCE
and KEINAN WARSAME

# MY FAVORITE THINGS
from THE SOUND OF MUSIC

OCARINA

Lyrics by OSCAR HAMMERSTEIN II
Music by RICHARD RODGERS

# OVER THE RAINBOW
from THE WIZARD OF OZ

OCARINA

Music by HAROLD ARLEN
Lyric by E.Y. "YIP" HARBURG

**Moderately, in 2**

# THE RAINBOW CONNECTION
from THE MUPPET MOVIE

OCARINA

Words and Music by PAUL WILLIAMS
and KENNETH L. ASCHER

# REINDEER(S) ARE BETTER THAN PEOPLE

from FROZEN

OCARINA

Music and Lyrics by KRISTEN ANDERSON-LOPEZ
and ROBERT LOPEZ

# SING
## from SESAME STREET

OCARINA

Words and Music by
JOE RAPOSO

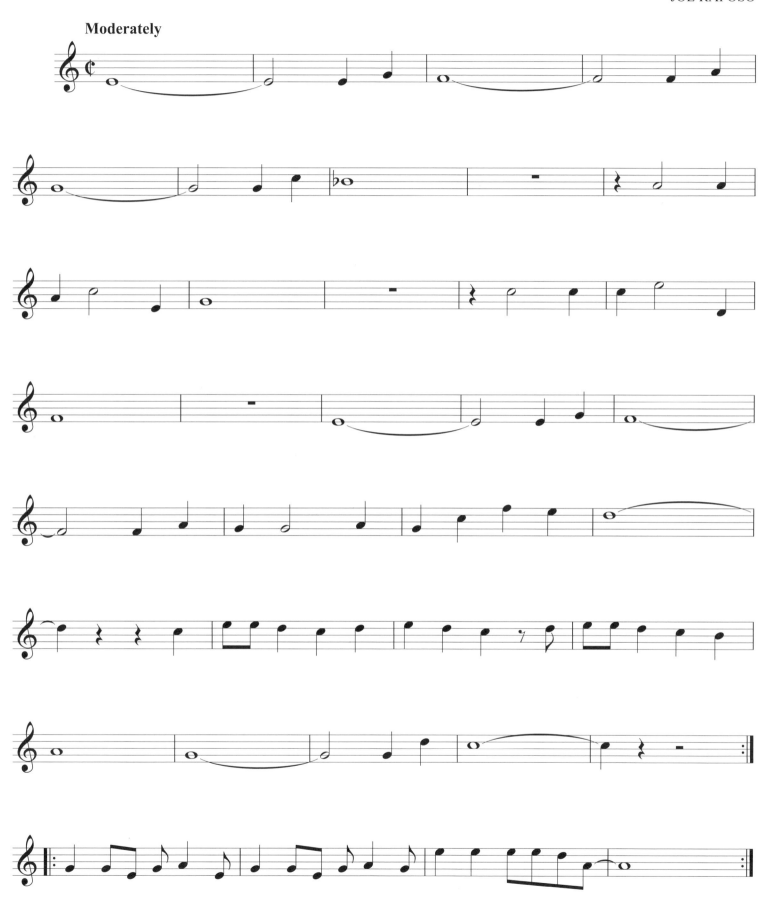

# SPLISH SPLASH

**OCARINA**

Words and Music by BOBBY DARIN
and MURRAY KAUFMAN

# A SPOONFUL OF SUGAR

from MARY POPPINS

OCARINA

Words and Music by RICHARD M. SHERMAN
and ROBERT B. SHERMAN

# THIS IS ME
## from THE GREATEST SHOWMAN

OCARINA

Words and Music by BENJ PASEK
and JUSTIN PAUL

# THIS LAND IS YOUR LAND

OCARINA

Words and Music by
WOODY GUTHRIE

Moderately bright

# TOMORROW
from the Musical Production ANNIE

OCARINA

Lyric by MARTIN CHARNIN
Music by CHARLES STROUSE

# YELLOW SUBMARINE

OCARINA

Words and Music by JOHN LENNON
and PAUL McCARTNEY

# WE DON'T TALK ABOUT BRUNO

from ENCANTO

OCARINA

Music and Lyrics by
LIN-MANUEL MIRANDA

**Moderate Cha-Cha**

# MORE GREAT OCARINA PUBLICATIONS

### Christmas Carols for Ocarina

*Arranged for 10, 11 & 12-Hole Ocarinas*

30 favorite carols of the holiday season: Angels We Have Heard on High • Away in a Manger • Coventry Carol • Deck the Hall • God Rest Ye Merry, Gentlemen • It Came upon the Midnight Clear • Jingle Bells • Joy to the World • O Come, All Ye Faithful • O Holy Night • Silent Night • Up on the Housetop • We Wish You a Merry Christmas • and more.

00277990 ..............................................$9.99

### Christmas Favorites for Ocarina

*Arranged for 10, 11 & 12-Hole Ocarinas*

Play 23 holiday classics in arrangements tailored to this unique wind instrument: Blue Christmas • Christmas Time Is Here • Do You Hear What I Hear • Frosty the Snow Man • Have Yourself a Merry Little Christmas • The Little Drummer Boy • The Most Wonderful Time of the Year • Rockin' Around the Christmas Tree • Silver Bells • White Christmas • Winter Wonderland • and more.

00277989 ..............................................$9.99

### Disney Songs for Ocarina

*Arranged for 10, 11 & 12-Hole Ocarinas*

30 Disney favorites, including: Be Our Guest • Can You Feel the Love Tonight • Colors of the Wind • Do You Want to Build a Snowman? • Evermore • He's a Pirate • How Far I'll Go • Kiss the Girl • Lava • Mickey Mouse March • Seize the Day • That's How You Know • When You Wish Upon a Star • A Whole New World • You've Got a Friend in Me • Zip-A-Dee-Doo-Dah • and more..

00275998 ........................................ $10.99

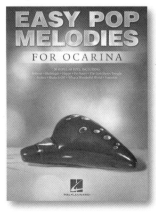

### Easy Pop Melodies for Ocarina

*Arranged for 10, 11 & 12-Hole Ocarinas*

30 popular hits: Believer • City of Stars • Every Breath You Take • Hallelujah • Happy • I'm Yours • The Lion Sleeps Tonight • My Heart Will Go on (Love Theme from *Titanic*) • Perfect • Rolling in the Deep • Shake It Off • Some Nights • The Sound of Silence • Stay with Me • Sweet Caroline • Uptown Girl • What a Wonderful World • Yesterday • You've Got a Friend • and more.

00275999 ........................................ $9.99

### Folk Songs for Ocarina

*Arranged for 10, 11 & 12-Hole Ocarinass*

41 well-known songs: Alouette • Aura Lee • The Banana Boat Song • Follow the Drinkin' Gourd • Frere Jacques (Are You Sleeping?) • Hava Nagila (Let's Be Happy) • Home on the Range • Hush, Little Baby • Joshua (Fit the Battle of Jericho) • Kumbaya • La Cucaracha • Loch Lomond • My Bonnie Lies over the Ocean • My Old Kentucky Home • My Wild Irish Rose • Oh! Susanna • Scarborough Fair • Shenandoah • Swing Low, Sweet Chariot • This Little Light of Mine • Twinkle, Twinkle Little Star • Volga Boatman Song • When Johnny Comes Marching Home • The Yellow Rose of Texas • and more.

00276000..............................................$9.99

### Hal Leonard Ocarina Method
#### by Cris Gale

The Hal Leonard Ocarina Method is a comprehensive, easy-to-use beginner's guide, designed for anyone just learning to play the ocarina. Inside you'll find loads of techniques, tips and fun songs to learn and play. The accompanying online video, featuring author Cris Gale, provides further instruction as well as demonstrations of the music in the book. Topics covered include: a history of the ocarina • types of ocarinas • breathing and articulation • note names and key signatures • meter signatures and rhythmic notation • fingering charts • many classic folksongs • and more.

00146676   Book/Online Video ....................................$14.99

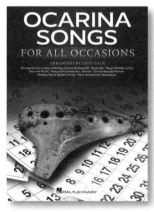

### Ocarina Songs for All Occasions

*Arranged for 10, 11 & 12-Hole Ocarinas*
#### arr. Cris Gale

30 songs for every season: America, the Beautiful • Auld Lang Syne • Danny Boy • Hail to the Chief • Happy Birthday to You • Joy to the World • The Old Rugged Cross • Pomp and Circumstance • Sevivon • The Star-Spangled Banner • Wedding March (Bridal Chorus) • When the Saints Go Marching In • and more.

00323196..............................................$9.99

### WWW.HALLEONARD.COM

*Prices, contents, and availability subject to change without notice.*
*Disney characters and artwork TM & © 2021 Disney*